Praise for *Border Song*

"Weisberg's deeply sad but heartfelt short book will haunt you long after you want it to, as you slowly realize that our American borders have become excruciating nightmares for migrants. He shares the chilling stories of artifacts left in the desert like black jugs, carpet shoes, bandanas, and an empty tin. This poignant book describes the border where there is no secure side to be on, no place to safely enter or exit. Weisberg refers to American songs and literature that remind us that perhaps the promise of freedom in America has been broken through these heart wrenching personal encounters and stories."

- Dr. Mehnaz Afridi, Manhattan College,
Shoah Through Muslim Eyes

"In Border Song, David Weisberg takes the reader on a journey with him along the Arizona-Mexico border. Weisberg writes beautifully about an ugly subject - our country's treatment of immigrants and asylum seekers seeking safety and a better life. As the leader of HIAS, the American Jewish community's agency for forcibly displaced persons, I am grateful that, by telling us what he sees, Weisberg makes the case for why Americans, particularly Jewish Americans, should care."

- Mark Hetfield,
President and CEO of HIAS

"David Weisberg loves turtles and, like the turtles in Mary Oliver's poem, knows that all things are 'tied to [him] by an unbreakable string.' Just as the protective turtle shell arches like the heavens, David brings us a vision of a world in which all are home wherever they are, in which all are sheltered."

- Rabbi Susan Silverman, *Casting Lots: Creating a Family in a Beautiful, Broken World*

Border Song

David Weisberg

Border Song

2020 Paperback Edition, *First Printing*
© 2020 David Weisberg
Introduction © 2020 Menachem Creditor
Cover Design: © 2020 Ben Kaplan

ISBN: 9798610472560

CONTENTS

Foreword

Walked out this morning, I don't believe what I saw. A hundred billion bottles washed up on the shore. Seems I'm not alone in being alone. A hundred billion castaways looking for a home.
- Sting

There are and will be scholarly books written about the migrant crisis at the U.S.-Mexico border. This is not one of those books.

I am not a scholar on this topic. I am not a journalist. I am not an expert.

Please don't use this book as your core source for a research paper. If my details are not all exactly right, they are to the best of my understanding and recollection.

But, I think, like many people, I am someone who has watched the migrant crisis from a distance and found myself feeling some combination of very troubled, deeply distressed, and completely powerless.

And, as I've gotten older (whether or not being in my fifties is "old," it's at least older), I've felt a spiritual drive in my gut that being concerned from a distance simply isn't good enough. So when I felt I'd recovered sufficiently from being a living liver donor six months earlier, I decided it was time to book a plane ticket to Tucson to take a deep dive into learning about the crisis and to see what kind of impact - if any - I might be able to make.

What I share with you in this book is not intended to be a detailed explanation of the crisis or of the failings of our immigration policy. It is not intended to be a political book either. While I certainly have my own (strong) political viewpoints, this is a tragedy where there seems to be plenty of blame to go around.

Instead, this is simply my travel blog, as I wrote it during my trip, with no intention at the time that it would be published as a book. I share with you what I experienced, as I experienced it, the stories I learned, and the feelings that I unpacked at the end of each physically, emotionally, and spiritually exhausting and often soul-crushing day.

While I shared my blog in real time with a small list of close friends, I am grateful to have the opportunity now to share it with you, as some combination of a message in a bottle - out there to be discovered - and a message on a billboard - shouted out in bold letters on the busiest of highways.

In doing so, I want to express my gratitude -

> - To the many wonderful people in Tucson who shepherded me through the desert and helped me to understand the crisis. I am inspired by your commitment.
> - To Rabbi Menachem Creditor, who read my blog, approached me about turning it into a book, partnered in publishing it, and was kind enough to write a beautiful introduction.
> - To my father, Joel Weisberg, who is my touchstone when it comes to seeking justice. As Dan Fogelberg wrote, "I'm just a living legacy to the leader of the band."
> - To my daughters, Hannah and Alison, who support and inspire me in every journey.

This book is dedicated to those I saw and met in places like Eloy Detention Center and Casa Alitas and the Evo Deconcini Federal Courthouse and to the many more that I didn't see, those running, those wandering, and those hiding, whether in Mexico, in the Sonoran Desert, or on a raft in the Mediterranean - all those castaways desperately seeking nothing more than a home.

To those of you choosing to read this book, thank you for doing your own part to learn, to care, and to make a difference.

I'll send an SOS to the world.
I hope that someone gets my
message in a bottle.

Introduction
Rabbi Menachem Creditor

*"Can this be true? This is the twentieth century,
not the Middle Ages. Who would allow
such crimes to be committed? How could
the world remain silent?"*
- Elie Wiesel, *Nobel Acceptance Speech (1986)*

The words of this book poured out of a sensitive, strong, wounded heart during the kind of experience Elie Wiesel called a "Kingdom of Darkness." That heart, David Weisberg's beautiful heart, created a work of testimony, a searing account of someone whose privilege made the journey into the heartbreaking world of refugees on the southern border of the United States, where untold numbers of scared people are trapped between barbed wire fences and denied basic human rights by the very nation whose founding Declaration of Independence castigated their British brethren of being "deaf to the voice of justice."

David's poetic testimony burns the soul and asks a similar question to the one Elie Wiesel posed in his 1986 speech in Oslo, upon accepting the Nobel Peace Prize. Wiesel shared with the audience of global dignitaries horrific stories from his younger years during the Shoah, and then channeled his childhood self's haunting question, posing it to himself and to the world:

> *"Tell me," he asks, "what have you done with my future, what have you done with your life?" And I tell him that I have tried. That I have tried to keep memory alive, that I have tried to fight those who would forget. Because if we forget, we are guilty, we are accomplices.*

The moral gauntlet has been thrown down too many times throughout our history to count. And, in this moment of rising nationalism, contagious dehumanization, political instability and sequestered living requires that we hear not only our inner wounded selves, the frightened children we never quite stop being, but the actual children and parents and grandparents at the border.

The particular method of the cry in your hands is also worthy of note: David's encyclopedic knowledge and felicitous use of prophetic song lyrics to deliver the harsh truths he encountered on his journey with grace and compassion. Music is a conduit for meaning, leading spiritual masters such as Rabbi Nachman of Breslov to nurture their students to listen closely to the world, since "each and every blade of grass has a song it likes to sing."[1]

So, dear friends, if even the grass' songs are audible, then the wind that carries them must be quite powerful. And if the wind is powerful enough to carry even those hidden sounds through the air, then hearing them is dependent upon our choice to listen for them. And if the difference between hearing and not-hearing is our decision to listen, how can we not hear the cries of the children whose journey through the wilderness has led them to the edges of our kingdom.

We can help. *But will we?* What will we do with the future? What will we do with our lives?

---

[1] Likutei Mohoran, Part II 63:1

The cries of the migrants are in the wind, and human kindness should know no border.

So this isn't quite a book. It is a primal cry to no longer turn a deaf ear to the real souls on our very real, and very sad, borders today.

To David should go our great thanks for expressing himself so skillfully, for being brave enough to make this journey, for the music of his soul, and for deciding that his own listening was only the beginning.

May we decide to hear as David has. May we do more than just listen; may we do everything in our power to change what is into something better, so that our sisters and brothers can finally sing a new song, a song of freedom. A song of coming home.

Rabbi Menachem Creditor
February 17, 2020

Border Song:
How I Plan to Spend
a Week in January
(December 17, 2019)

*Let us strive to find a way to make all hatred cease.
There's a man over there, what's his color I don't
care. He's my brother let us live in peace.*
- Elton John, Border Song

As we finish the last couple weeks of 2019, it's been a profound year for me, as I was able to complete my dream of being a living liver donor. Getting a chance to develop a relationship with my liver recipient, Joe, and knowing that he's doing so well, has been powerful and rewarding. And my recovery has far exceeded my expectations. In fact, I've come to tell folks lately that, if I didn't have a scar, you might be able to convince me that the whole thing never happened, as those days in the hospital are in many ways just a blur at this point.

One thing that I didn't do last year was any significant travel. I had originally planned to go to Uganda in October, with the intent of seeing gorillas, meeting with the Abayudaya Jewish community, and seeing a water project in a displaced persons' camp that our community helped to fund. But once my liver donation surgery was scheduled for July, it felt like it wouldn't be the most prudent choice to schedule that kind of travel. (Had I known how quickly I would recover, I would probably have gone, but for now I have that on the backburner, perhaps for late 2020.)

With the new year coming, however, I've been yearning to return to some impactful travel once again. My original intention was that I might spend a week in Central America in January volunteering with sea turtle rescue efforts. Anyone who knows me well (or has ever stepped foot in my home) knows that I love turtles. But, as it turns out, January isn't a good time for the turtles, and they weren't willing to change their mating or migration times to suit my travel schedule.

As I tried to think of meaningful alternatives for spending an impactful week, another idea occurred to me.

For several years, I, like so many others, have watched with deep concern - but at a great distance - the migrant crisis at the U.S.-Mexico border. Regardless of politics, I'm not sure anyone disagrees that there is a significant crisis. But, for so many of us, it's a nameless, faceless crisis. It's about a mass of people, but it's not about individuals and families with stories, with hopes and fears and dreams and realities.

I decided that I want to make my own effort to change that. Both to make a modest but meaningful impact where I can and to begin to put some names and faces and stories on the crisis.

And so, in mid-January, I am going to take a week of vacation and fly to Tucson, Arizona to work with non-profits engaged with the migrant crisis and, I hope, to meet some of the people whose lives literally hang in the balance. I started reaching out to organizations in late November, and I began to make contacts and put together a plan.

As I begin to flesh out my schedule for the week, it already includes two trips with the organization Humane Borders to fill water stations in the desert for those on the journey, gleaning produce with migrants with a non-profit called Iskashitaa, bearing witness for those in court regarding a program called Operation Streamline, serving dinner at a migrant shelter in Tucson called Casa Alitas, and potentially volunteering with an organization called Scholarships A to Z focused on making higher education accessible to all, regardless of immigration status. I'm also trying to arrange to visit a detention center, and I hope to spend a day volunteering in Nogales, Mexico, perhaps working at a soup kitchen.

In addition to making an impact on the ground there, my intent is to blog my trip (starting with this note) and then come back and speak about it in my community, hopefully putting names and faces on this otherwise nameless and faceless humanitarian crisis.

As I move forward in my planning and then on my trip, I look forward to the opportunity to take you along on this journey with me. Although I wish there wasn't a crisis to see, it is my hope that I can share with you stories and photos of what I experience. If you have questions that you'd like me to try to answer on this journey or suggestions of places to go, people to meet, or organizations with which to interact, I am always happy to hear from you.

While my liver donation process was dedicated to my mother, this journey I am dedicating to my father, inspired by his journey several years ago, then at age 75, to support those involved in the protests at Standing Rock in the Dakotas. My father for me has always been the touchstone when it comes to pursuing justice, and it is his life model that guides me on this trip.

Let us - *and all* - live in peace.

Border Song:
Packing My Adjectives
(January 16, 2020)

*We barely had arrived. Friends asked us to describe
the people, places, and every last thing. So we
unpacked our adjectives.*
- from *Unpack Your Adjectives,*
George R. Newall (Schoolhouse Rock)

When you haven't been planning a trip for too long, it's a different kind of anticipation. It was just last month that I began thinking about a trip to the U.S.-Mexico border to get a firsthand view of the migrant crisis and to see what kind of impact I could make as a volunteer; and I'm leaving for Tucson this afternoon.

But I'm not sure it's the timeframe that's had the greatest effect on my anticipation, as, rarely at a loss for words, I've found myself challenged to describe my feelings entering this journey. Descriptors such as "excited" or "anxious," which I might have used at the beginning of my blogs for my journey to my ancestral village in Ukraine or my liver donation, don't seem at all appropriate. "Curious" seems way too flippant, especially as I leave for a trip driven by a situation that I wish didn't exist to be seen at all.

And so, as I packed my bags for this trip, I heeded the lessons I learned from Schoolhouse Rock cartoon shorts as a child and thought about how I might pack my adjectives.

If forced to unpack one of those adjectives now to describe my feelings leaving on this journey, I suppose the best choice would be "motivated" - motivated to learn, motivated to put names and faces and stories on a crisis that I've only heard about through the media and from a great distance, motivated to share those learnings and stories with others, motivated to discover how I might make any impact, both on the ground and back at home.

Unlike my recent trips and experiences, and despite having a pretty full schedule planned, I enter this journey having little idea what it is I will see or experience and how I might walk away feeling - sad, angry, frustrated, inspired, depressed, helpless, most likely some combination of all of those and beyond.

But I do know that I go into this journey already grateful to many wonderful people in Tucson who have never met me but have helped to shape my itinerary for the week - staff and volunteers of more than a half-dozen local non-profits who have enabled me to do everything from refilling water stations in the desert to visiting a migrant detention center and seeing the border wall. I could not be doing this without their support, and I am already in awe of what is clear they do for so many others and for which I hope, if even in just a small way, I can help to shoulder the burden.

I've become increasingly aware, since I began planning this trip, of the decreasing frequency with which I hear about the migrant crisis in the news, not because it has diminished in any way, but because we're living in a moment where each day seems to bring a new crisis that - sometimes seemingly intentionally - sends a fog over the prior one. Meanwhile, within that haze, people continue to live and die in desperation. To paraphrase Joni Mitchell, I am going there to lose the smog and (I hope) to be a cog in something turning.

I am an absolute believer that things happen for a reason, and it provided an incredibly helpful context for me that I spent this past week hosting my dear friend, Qes Efraim Zion-Lawi, an Ethiopian Jewish spiritual leader from Israel. Qes Efraim's parents were themselves refugees some 40 years ago, walking 500 miles in bare feet from Ethiopia to Sudan, spending 11 months in a Red Cross refugee camp being told they needed to hide their identity or face grave consequences, and having a nine-year-old daughter die in that refugee camp before they were finally airlifted to safety and a new home in Israel.

The story of Qes Efraim's family these past days becomes my entry point as I get ready to see, to meet, and, I hope, to provide some support and comfort to those making their own exodus, perhaps from violence in Guatemala, El Salvador, or Honduras, traveling 2,000 or more miles, searching and yearning for safety, security, hope, and home.

As I search for and unpack my adjectives this week, I'll be ever mindful of that other lesson I learned from Schoolhouse Rock, the one about lovely Lady Liberty and her book of recipes, the one that provided a new life for my Bubby Naomi and Zayde Charlie whose village of Obodivka I visited two years ago, and the great American melting pot I dream we can and should still be. And I'll take you along with me each day, hoping that what I learn and experience and the adjectives I unpack to describe it can have an impact on all of us.

You simply melt right in. It doesn't matter what your skin. It doesn't matter where you're from, or your religion, you jump right into the great American melting pot.
- from *The Great American Melting Pot,*
Lynn Ahrens (Schoolhouse Rock)

Border Song:
Water, Water, Everywhere,
Nor Any Drop to Drink
(January 17, 2020)

I arrived at my AirBNB at roughly 1:15 am, only half cursing myself for having signed up for a water run with an organization called Humane Borders that required I report to their location in Tucson by 6 am. It was only a day or so ago that I realized I had managed to book myself a place to stay nearly 30 minutes outside of downtown Tucson, meaning that I set my alarm to wake me up at 4:45 am this morning so that I could be there on time. I probably got a cumulative two hours of sleep last night once I finally settled in. And I woke up this morning at 4:30 am, ahead of my alarm and running on adrenaline.

Those who know me well know that I am almost always early. True to form, I was outside the Humane Borders truck lot at 5:45 am, and there I sat waiting for others to arrive, including the driver leading the trip where we were scheduled to spend the day filling water stations for migrants in the Buenos Aires National Wildlife Refuge. And I waited, and I waited, wondering if I was in the wrong location, even though I parked right next to the murals that were specifically printed on my directions for the day. By 6 am, I thought I needed to reach out to the driver. By 6:15 am, I thought I needed to reach out to the administrative coordinator for Humane Borders.

Finally, I received a text. *The run was canceled last night - did your driver not contact you?*

Accidents and miscommunications happen. Sure, I was annoyed, but I allowed that to pass. There were more important things to do today than be angry at kind people who dedicate their lives to doing good things. I learned that the run to deliver water in the middle of the desert needed to be canceled because heavy rain last night made the roads in the wildlife refuge simply not passable. The irony wasn't lost on me. As Samuel Taylor Coleridge wrote in *The Rime of the Ancient Mariner* (and I'll admit, I had misremembered it as a line from

Shakespeare until I Googled it) "Water, water, everywhere, nor any drop to drink."

Fortunately, Rebecca from Humane Borders was keenly aware of my disappointment and my desire to jump quickly into learning about and making some impact with regard to the migrant crisis. She let me know there was another group leaving this morning from an organization called Tucson Samaritans. They would also be going into the desert with water and other supplies for migrants, but they would be going to a different location and their vehicles were much lighter so the roads wouldn't be as much of an issue. The trip was leaving at 7:30 am from another location near where I was. Rebecca even decided to join me.

So perhaps I could have gotten another 90 minutes sleep, although, quite honestly, I had woken up on my own at 4:30 am, still on East Coast time. More importantly, I was moving forward with my journey, and, if I had gotten the message last night about the Humane Borders trip being cancelled, I might not ever have found out about this other opportunity.

I met Rebecca, Sarah, Jim, and Hilton at the Tucson Samaritans meeting spot and storage shed. Rebecca, Sarah, and Jim have decades of experience in this volunteer work. They are part of an amazing local community of volunteers dedicated to helping the migrant population. Hilton, like me, was there on a first-time experience, although her grandmother (who I had the opportunity to meet) is apparently a legendary volunteer in the movement.

A major difference between Humane Borders and Tucson Samaritans seems to be that Humane Borders takes large barrels of water to refill major water stations at fixed locations in the desert. Tucson Samaritans, on the other hand, takes gallon jugs of water, along with blankets, food packages, and so on. The jugs are left at strategic places where they might be found by those in need. The blankets and food packages are distributed if there is a direct encounter with a migrant who needs them. We filled up the four-wheel-drive SUV with all of these supplies, and we headed out to the desert.

A quick, funny note is that Tucson Samaritans has two vehicles, and each has a name. We were in Josephine today, but Josephine's sibling vehicle is named Joe, after the infamous Sheriff Joe Arpaio - not in his honor but instead because it was purchased with moneys from the settlement of a lawsuit by a local journalist against Sheriff Joe.

I was curious as to what the likelihood was that we would encounter migrants walking through the desert. Jim told me that while those encounters happen, and every regular volunteer has had them, they don't happen with great regularity. Having gone into this experience not sure what to expect, I had to quickly remind myself - in the crudest way - that this wasn't a safari or a whale-watching expedition. It wasn't about having a sighting; it was about leaving life-saving resources for people in desperate need.

Our drive today took us to the Ironwood Forest National Monument area of the desert. The area is actually north of Tucson, roughly 50 miles from the Mexico border. I asked why migrants would be so far north, and I was told that those here were unlikely seeking asylum (as those seeking asylum turn themselves in as soon as they cross the border) but instead, more likely, those who had been deported and were trying to get back to their families.

The desert was cold in the morning. When we reached our destination, and when the SUV could go no further (because the roads weren't in great shape at Ironwood either), we switched to walking. Each of us carried gallon jugs of water, and I put a couple food packages in my backpack just in case we found someone in need.

We did see a couple of artifacts from migrants while we were walking. An empty tuna can. A used water jug. But, in the broad Arizona daylight, we saw no migrants. My understanding is, just like in the stories I have heard from my friends who made the exodus from Ethiopia to Sudan about walking at night and hiding during the day, it is best to not be visible. This was underscored overhead by the U.S. Border Patrol helicopter that we saw flying above us, scanning the ground.

There was some contrast in the ugliness of the circumstances that led me to visit the

Sonoran Desert today for the very first time, and the sheer beauty of the environment itself. At times, I felt like I was walking in a giant terrarium. It could be easy to simply be lost in the beauty of it all, were this not a place also filled with such sadness.

As we hiked further, Rebecca showed me that her handheld GPS had a category on it to identify RHRs. Yes, we were there to leave supplies that sustain life because migrants die in the desert. RHR stands for *recovered human remains*. There have been enough of those discoveries that the GPS has a listing for them. Rebecca, Sarah, and Jim told me they had all been on missions to search for those presumed dead, and they had each been involved in making such a grim discovery.

We walked to one of those sites - a small cross marking where they had discovered the remains of Prudencia Martin Gomez, an 18-year-old woman from Guatemala who died in the desert trying to reunite with her boyfriend, who had fled violence in their home country. I am told that when they found her remains, much of them had been picked apart and scattered by wild animals. Each of us paid our respects there in our own way. And we left some water jugs by the site, such that anyone in a similarly desperate situation as Prudencia would have water to drink.

There had been a bandana on a tree right next to Prudencia's memorial which helped to mark the site, but the bandana has become quite worn and barely recognizable. For some reason, I had thrown a blue bandana into my backpack this morning when I packed for the day. I took out the bandana and tied it to a high branch of the tree, leaving it behind as a sign to anyone passing that there was water nearby.

On our drive out, Rebecca's eye caught an artifact by the side of the road, and Jim quickly stopped the vehicle. It was a black colored water jug (unlike ours, which were transparent). Rebecca explained that the black water jugs come from Mexico and are used because they aren't reflective, making them less likely to be spotted by Border Patrol when being carried by someone making the journey. When Rebecca examined the water jug, she noticed a slit in the side of it. Her educated guess was that

Border Patrol had found the jug and destroyed it, and perhaps the migrant carrying it had been apprehended.

When we left, the desert was hot, sunny, and dry. The wet roads from last night were drying up. And the water we left behind sits waiting, flanked by a blue bandana and a small wooden cross.

Border Song:
A Day of Difficult Truths
(January 18, 2020)

I came to Tucson wanting to learn about the migrant crisis, and I had no doubt that would require hearing difficult truths. I'm not sure I properly anticipated how many and how difficult those truths would be.

I hesitate to use the word *serendipity*, which inherently implies something happy, but it was a helpful accident that my visit to Tucson coincided with the Border Issues Fair, a once-a-year event coordinated by the Good Shepherd United Church of Christ in Sahuarita, just south of the city. That's where I found myself this morning. Of course, I was one of the first participants there, well before the starting time.

The Border Issues Fair features both keynote speakers and tables from many of the local organizations involved in providing support to migrants (many of those organizations already being on my schedule for the week), and I was grateful that, in one place, I would have the opportunity to hear from and speak to so many people.

Arriving before the speakers started, I wandered to the area in which tables were being set up, and I was drawn to a table with all kinds of Central American crafts for sale, including some small turtles. (For those who don't know, I collect turtle figurines, and have well over one hundred in my home. I can't resist a table with turtles for sale.) I noticed that the table wasn't simply about selling turtles or other crafts, but was also collecting donations and included a photo of a young boy that said "Seeking Justice for José Antonio Elena Rodriguez." I needed to know more, and Anna Maria, who was behind the table, passionately obliged, telling me the story of José, who in 2012 at age 16 was shot and killed by U.S. Border Patrol. She told me that over 100 people have been killed by Border Patrol, but, in José's rare case - as with several others - while the bullets were fired from the U.S., José was struck on the other side of the border, in Mexico, with 16 shots in 34 seconds. Border Patrol, Anna Maria told me, are never found guilty of criminal charges. But, because José was in

Mexico and this is considered a transnational killing, his family is also denied any rights to a civil suit. A case is now coming to the U.S. Supreme Court on this issue. By Anna Maria's table hung a banner, documenting the pictures and names of over a dozen migrants seeking asylum who were killed by Border Patrol. She gave me a poster of José and asked if I could hold a vigil in my community for him, as she does on the 10th of every month. I donated some money to the cause (as I wanted to for every organization I met today), and I bought a small turtle.

It was a jarring way to begin the day; and it was an appropriate prologue for the learning to come.

When I went into the sanctuary to hear the keynote speakers, it was a full house, with those showing up at the last minute (never me) scrambling to find the remaining seats. I estimated likely 250-300 people there, and, while I was inspired to see so many people dedicated to the cause, I was somewhat disappointed or confused, in my early fifties, that clearly 90% of those in attendance were older than I am. I'm hopeful that's only a reflection of the older

Tucson demographic and not interest in and passion for migrant rights.

There were three speakers today, the first being Sebastian Quinac, who, born in Guatemala, sought asylum in the U.S. fleeing death threats in his country and is now an advocate for asylum seekers. He explained that, with recent changes in immigration policy from the current administration, those coming from Guatemala to the U.S. and seeking asylum are now given two choices - wait in Mexico (where it's dangerous) or go back home to Guatemala (where it's even more dangerous). This is what's called the MPP, the Migrant Protection Protocols, which seem to provide just the opposite of protection. The unofficial name for this policy is the "Remain in Mexico" program, implemented in January 2019. The policy forces asylum seekers traveling through Mexico from other Central American countries - most typically those fleeing violence in Guatemala, Honduras, or El Salvador - to stay in Mexico during the immigration proceedings, which can take up to two years. Tens of thousands of asylum seekers have been returned to Mexico through this program, including close to 20,000 children and over 500 infants. Many of those returned have been victims of rape, kidnapping, torture, extortion, and more. Sebastian also explained the language barriers in the asylum system, as many of those arriving at the border do not speak Spanish, but instead speak one of a large number of indigenous languages for which there are not ready translators. Sebastian himself serves as a translator of the Kachiquel language, but he explained that many of those seeking asylum are denied rights simply because they don't understand what is being said to them and many have no idea why they are being held in detention.

We then heard from Todd Miller, a journalist and author, who has traveled the world investigating border issues and enforcement policies. Todd explained how it is current U.S. strategy to stop asylum-seekers well before they reach the U.S. border. He spoke of an earthquake in Haiti, where U.S. ships were sent to the Haitian coast to make announcements that anyone who attempted to come to the U.S. for refuge would immediately be sent home, and how John Kelly, as Department of

Homeland Security Secretary, had stated that security begins 1,500 miles from the U.S. border in Peru (which Todd jokingly pointed out is much further than 1,500 miles away). He also helped us understand how U.S. border security has become an exportable industry around the world, a big business with technologies being sold to other countries trying to deny refugees entry. Todd talked of attending border patrol innovations trade shows around the world, including one that showcased a robot that could be equipped with a handgun, sighted using a remote control, as well as the use of drone technologies for border patrol.

Having come out of my liver donation journey just six months ago feeling inspired by the power of humanity and technology working hand-in-hand, my heart sank to realize technology isn't on the same side of the humanity that sat with me in that church sanctuary today. And I fear that the technology will always and increasingly be stronger than good wills and kind hearts.

Our third speaker was Francesco Piobbichi, a fine artist and an organizer for Mediterranean Hope, an immigration project of the Waldensian Church in Italy that focuses on migrants in the Mediterranean. With the assistance of translators, Francesco told heart-breaking stories of refugees from Syria and Libya, illuminated by his beautiful and poignant drawings. I purchased one of his prints that particularly touched me, of a boy sitting by a border fence in Libya, while an oil pipeline runs right through to the other side of the border. Francesco was clear in his remarks, "The border is everywhere, and it's a border against poor people." I was moved when he cited Jewish texts at the end of his talk, quoting "To save one life is to save an entire world," and then adding "...whether in the ocean or in the desert."

I left the Border Issues Fair feeling both sad and inspired, both overwhelmed and enriched. And knowing that the day wasn't going to become easier.

This afternoon, I met with Jill Rich, a member of the local Jewish Community Relations Council, and one of the leaders in the Tucson Jewish community's involvement with supporting the migrant community. Our plan a week ago was for Jill to take me to Casa Alitas, a local migrant shelter, where we would help serve dinner together to the residents. But Jill called me a few days ago and told me that we'd no longer be needed to help serve dinner. While Casa Alitas typically has around 150 migrants in shelter, recent enforcement of the Remain in Mexico policy meant that those coming across the border seeking asylum were being immediately sent to El Paso and then back over the border to Mexico. There were few people at Casa Alitas these days, and they wouldn't need our support with dinner. Still, she said, she'd arrange for me to have a tour.

I quickly realized when we met just how little I know about the asylum system. What happens when someone is seeking asylum? Who would be staying at Casa Alitas?

What I learned - and this is my understanding of things - is that those who cross the border and seek asylum, if they aren't just sent back to Mexico, are first held in U.S. Immigration and Customs Enforcement (ICE) detention facilities at the border where they have an opportunity to apply for asylum, which must be reviewed by an asylum officer and then a judge. Typically those first applications happen without any legal representation. It is at those ICE detention facilities that family separation happens and those horrific children-in-cages stories occur. If one is approved to have the opportunity to seek asylum, they can be released from ICE detention if they have a sponsor (usually a family member) who is willing to house and care for them until their asylum hearing (which can be approximately two years away). Those who don't have a sponsor remain in ICE detention, in harsh facilities, often for long periods of time. Some opt simply to leave and go back home. Those who have a sponsor are delivered by ICE to facilities such as Casa Alitas. (They had previously simply been left at the Greyhound bus station in Tucson, but it was agreed that was a problem for all parties, and ICE now cooperates in delivering people to places like Casa Alitas.)

Casa Alitas is a partnership between Pima County, Catholic Social Services, and, to some extent, the Jewish Federation. I was proud and grateful to learn of the Jewish community's involvement and support in these efforts. The purpose of shelters like

Casa Alitas is to provide short-term shelter, medical care, clothing, food, and travel coordination to help asylum seekers reach their sponsors. On my tour, I was shown the room where travel coordination is done, and I saw a screen showing the transports that had been initiated that day, including to Los Angeles, Atlanta, New Orleans, and Minneapolis. The typical stay at Casa Alitas is just two or three nights.

There was something both comforting and startling about Casa Alitas, which was started in a home, moved to a monastery when the population became too large, and now is housed in what was formerly a county juvenile detention facility. While the entryway is bright and colorful and there are common spaces with toys and art supplies and a sofa and TV watching area, the rooms that those in the shelter sleep in at night are still the rather cold-looking rooms of a juvenile detention facility. But I imagine there's a sense of security within those walls, knowing that you have the freedom to step outside them into community, and it's a far cry from the ICE detention facilities that those in Casa Alitas have just left. I can only imagine it feels like a godsend after the trauma of making an exodus from a violent homeland and being held in ICE detention.

And I did see some families there - two parents with a child from Honduras, a mother and daughter from Guatemala, and others. Hugo, my tour guide, explained to me that, in the case of the mother and daughter, the father had been taken away as part of the family separation policy and sent to a detention facility in Mississippi, a place with a reputation, Hugo said, of being quite brutal. While many families are reunited, he had grave doubts in this case that the mother and daughter would ever see the father again.

Hugo was open in answering my questions with great transparency. I asked about the percentage of those who are granted the opportunity to seek asylum that will actually be approved. I anticipated a high percentage, considering they had already been approved to apply. Hugo responded: 1%. That means, of the twenty-some people whom I saw at Casa Alitas today, it is entirely likely that all will be denied asylum and sent back to dangerous situations in their home countries. It is for that reason, Jill later explained to me, that many of those approved to seek asylum simply don't show up for their hearings. It's safer to hide than to appear at a hearing and risk being sent back home.

It was a day of difficult truths. While I am so deeply inspired by the many organizations and the incredible volunteers who give of their time, energy, hearts, and wallets to provide support for those seeking asylum, the obstacles - politics, policy, poverty, prejudice, and technology - can feel almost insurmountable.

As I drove back to my own comfortable shelter for the night, I did my best to try to let the inspiration outweigh the sense of despair. Driving with the desert by my side, I saw something flying over the road in front of me.

From the distance I first thought it was a helicopter. Then I smiled, realizing it was likely a hawk.

As I got closer, the drone crossed the highway in front of me and over the desert, its eye focused on the ground below, mine opened to the difficult truths here by the border.

Border Song:
Who Do We Call the Enemy?
(January 19, 2020)

Who do we call the enemy? My children, my children. Who do we call the enemy? Who do we call the enemy? The enemy is poverty, and the wall keeps out the enemy, and we build the wall to keep us free. That's why we build the wall. We build the wall to keep us free.
- Anaïs Mitchell

Rick and Ellen spend half their time in Seattle and half their time - the winter, of course - in Tucson. When I met them in the Borderlinks parking lot this morning to go on a Tucson Samaritans trip, I felt like we clicked right away. They are friendly, charitable, committed people who dedicate a great deal of their lives to supporting the migrant community. And it didn't hurt that Rick was wearing a Keith Haring sweatshirt. (I am a huge Keith Haring fan.)

While we spoke about many of the harsh realities of the migrant crisis during our drive south, it was generally a positive and uplifting conversation.

And then we entered Nogales, Arizona, turned a corner, and there it was. We were driving along the border wall separating Nogales, Arizona from Nogales, Mexico. Not a new "We're going to build a wall" wall, but instead, one that has clearly existed for some time, although Ellen told me that there have been recent modifications, such as wire mesh fencing that now runs across the wall covering the gaps between the slats of fence. She said that people used to hold hands from one side of the wall to the other; apparently that was deemed some kind of threat.

The border wall, as it exists in Nogales - which is certainly not indicative of the entire U.S.-Mexico border - is cold and menacing, with several serpentine strands of shiny and sharp steel barbed wire. Unlike other border walls or separation barriers that I have seen that are solid, it feels almost cruel to be able to see through, a tease to what's on the other side, and not the same canvas for murals and protest graffiti as I know from other places. As we drove along the wall, we saw Border Patrol vehicles and surveillance towers, an indication that the wall may not be believed to be impenetrable, despite its height, strength, and razor-like extensions.

We stopped, and Rick pointed out to me the place that José Antonio Elena Rodriguez had been shot 16 times and killed by Border Patrol while standing in Mexico, allegedly for throwing rocks. There is such a drop in the spot from the U.S. side of the fence to the Mexican side that it's hard to believe anyone could be throwing rocks over it from the Mexican side, and particularly in a way that was at all menacing and would require lethal self-defense.

I'm told that Nogales used to feel like one big town spanning the U.S. and Mexican sides. That's now long gone, a separation that has had a severe economic impact on the much smaller Arizona Nogales, while the Mexico Nogales has become overrun with cartels, of which I'll say more soon.

Ellen and Rick drove me to see the Nogales border crossing where, among other things, one can see deportations happen on an almost daily basis. Busses, I'm told, are driven to the border, where those being deported are taken out, unshackled (yes, they are taken in chains), and sent back to the other side of the border. They told me they've even seen busses of children deported, "unaccompanied minors," as they are called. We didn't see any deportations today, as apparently, Sunday is deportation-free.

I am considering whether I might come back when I have some free time on Wednesday morning and cross the border into Nogales to witness the situation on the other side. While I might, Ellen and Rick warned me that, depending upon the lines, it might be a long wait to get back into the U.S., as Border Patrol takes their time in processing those whose profile might indicate a Mexican or Central American nationality. It could take hours to get back through the border.

From the startling coldness of the wall, on what was a chilly morning, we headed on a Tucson Samaritans run to Walker Canyon, much closer to the border than the run I had taken on Friday to Ironwood and a much, much different environment, as sand and saguaros were replaced with rocks, mud, trees, and brush. Almost immediately after we stepped out of the car, Rick made a discovery that was familiar to him but something I had never seen before.

By the side of the road, Rick discovered a small gathering of carpet shoes - shoes with a sole made from carpeting such that they won't leave tracks on the ground. These are a valuable tool for those trying to surreptitiously make their way through the canyon without the notice of Border Patrol.

While carpet shoes used to be handmade and quite rudimentary, these shoes were fairly uniform and well made. Rick told me that's because the cartels - organized crime syndicates on the other side of the border - now forbid migrants from making their own necessities for their journey, instead requiring that everything be purchased from the cartels, a small piece of massive extortion imposed by the cartels on desperate migrants. Indeed, the black water jugs like the one we found in Ironwood also must be purchased exclusively from the cartels.

In addition to their business of drug smuggling, the cartels have developed an industry of preying upon migrants. In order to get to and cross the border, you need to pay up.

And so the obstacles that exist once someone gets across the border - harsh terrain and weather, detention, family separation, denial of asylum, deportation, and so on, are just the final indignities in a nightmarish odyssey that begins with constant threats of violence, rape, kidnapping, and robbery along the journey, massive extortion from the cartels, and the great likelihood of being denied asylum and sent back home on the small chance one is able to cross the border in the first place. Knowing how terrifying that journey must be - especially for a young family with multiple children - one has to imagine that the situation in their home countries that they are running from must be absolutely hellish; and most end up right back where they started, looking to start the whole process over again for the same hope of finding a new life in what they believe to be a land of opportunity.

Indeed, while there is a wall, it doesn't separate safety from danger, it doesn't separate opportunity from desperation, it doesn't separate decency from corruption. Danger, desperation, and corruption flourish freely on all sides, a serpentine of barbed wire that begins in Central America and doesn't end at the U.S. border.

Ellen, Rick, and I saw a few more artifacts on our hike through Walker Canyon. We saw footprints heading north (presumably from those without carpet shoes) and empty water jugs from previous drops. At one point, Rick sensed there might be some migrants in the area, and he yelled out in Spanish, "We are friendly, and we are bringing you water." Nobody emerged, not surprisingly. Even if there were migrants hiding, I wondered if a Border Patrol agent might be just as likely to yell out Rick's friendly message, hoping it might lure out someone seeking help.

After I said goodbye to Ellen and Rick, I went to do something different this afternoon, as I had heard at the Border Issues Fair about a group of copper miners who were on strike just south of Tucson. American workers, they are on strike against ASARCO, a subsidiary of Grupo Mexico, a leading global company in copper production, a Mexican company that they feel is denying them proper wages and benefits. The strike has now gone on for over three months, and the striking workers are suffering. I learned that a group was planning to stand in solidarity with the copper miners this afternoon, singing union songs in support of their effort. I wanted to be a part of that.

At the copper mine strike site, I saw a number of people that I had seen just yesterday at the Border Issues Fair. As we sang our way through the great list of workers'-rights songs, we joined over voices together for "Which Side Are You On?"

> *"My daddy was a miner, and I'm a miner's son. He'll be with you fellow workers until this battle's won. Which side are you on? Which side are you on? Which side are you on? Which side are you on?"* - Florence Reece

I find myself on the side of the migrants and the copper miners.

But, as I discovered today, when it comes to the border wall, there are really no good sides at all.

Border Song:
You May Say I'm a Dreamer
(January 20, 2020)

You may say I'm a dreamer,
but I'm not the only one.
I hope someday you'll join us,
and the world will live as one.
- John Lennon

My previous two visits to Mexico had been short shopping trips to Tijuana - perhaps a few hours long - when I happened to be in San Diego or Los Angeles. It would have been reasonable to assume that my next time in Mexico would be more substantial.

Not today.

I met Dennis at the Humane Borders truck lot at 7 am this morning to join him on the Sasabe water run. Humane Borders is different from the previous water runs that I joined from Tucson Samaritans, in that Humane Borders is carrying very large barrels of water to specific stations. And the Sasabe run is the simplest.

When I arrived, the truck was already loaded up with a 300-gallon tank of fresh drinking water. Our assignment - one that Dennis does every week - was simple. Drive the water to Sasabe, Mexico, about 90 minutes away, and transfer the water to Grupos Beta, the humanitarian arm of the Mexican government, who would then distribute the water to various staging sites that serve migrants.

And as simple as it sounds is as simple as it was. We drove to Sasabe, Arizona, were waved right through the border control (where there were no others cars in line), drove maybe 20 yards into Mexico, turned right in the Grupos Beta lot, ran a hose from our tank to theirs, turned on a pump, and waited 45 minutes for the transfer to be complete. When our water tank was empty and theirs was full, we rolled up the hose, jumped back in the truck, drove the minute it took to get back to U.S. border control, showed our passports (we weren't even asked for them when we were entering Mexico), and headed back to Tucson.

A short, uneventful 45-minute trip about 20 yards into Mexico.

And, for Dario, that brief step into Mexico could be enough the remove his right to work and take away his driver's license.

Dario and Zobella, whom I met with this afternoon, are both volunteers with the Tucson-based non-profit Scholarships A-Z.

Zobella, 27, is a non-Latino, American citizen, who has a passion for immigrants' rights. Dario, 25, was born in Mexico, is undocumented, and presently has the status of being a DACA recipient under the Deferred Action for Childhood Arrivals program.

Why I instinctively referred to Dario as a "dreamer," thinking it synonymous with DACA recipients, Dario clarified that the term "dreamer" has been used since long before DACA to talk about undocumented youth or undocumented students; and since DACA isn't a permanent solution, DACA recipients have also been lumped under the "dreamers" term.

Dario chooses to identify as a DACA recipient. And Dario, along with so many other undocumented young people, has dreams.

Dario was able to apply for and be approved as a DACA recipient because he meets a complicated set of criteria defined by the executive order that created the program in 2012. Those criteria include having entered the country before one's 16th birthday; having lived continuously in the U.S. since June 2007; being under age 31 on June 2012; having completed high school or a GED; and more. And being a DACA recipient has brought with it some significant benefits, including the opportunity to get a work permit and a driver's license. As a DACA recipient, Dario now has a Social Security number, something he hadn't had for his entire life. Perhaps most importantly, being a recipient has allowed Dario to work as a graduate assistant at the University of Arizona, which in turn pays for his education.

And many things could risk that status, including leaving the country without prior approval from the Department of

Homeland Security, even for a 45-minute trip to Mexico. And, regardless of anything Dario might do, the potential expiration of DACA lies ahead, which would suddenly strip him and fellow recipients of the opportunities afforded them by the program. In fact, with DACA status lasting for two years and requiring renewal, Dario and Zobella told me that they are encouraging recipients to renew now, even if their status is not up yet, due to what have become lengthy renewal times, as well as attempts by the present U.S. administration to raise the application fee from $495 to $795.

Scholarships A-Z was formed over ten years ago and, to date, has been entirely volunteer-led (although there is a plan to soon hire their first-ever paid executive director). Their mission is a simple one - to provide resources and scholarships to students, families, and educators through online and community interactions, in order to make higher education accessible to all, regardless of immigration status.

Those who are undocumented are ineligible for state tuition rates for colleges and universities and ineligible for state and federal financial aid (although it differs from state to state, that is the case in Arizona). And so providing educational opportunity that enables young undocumented students (and not just DACA recipients) to succeed is a major uphill battle. For Scholarships A-Z that started with simply creating a website of private scholarships for which undocumented applicants are eligible. They soon found that website was being accessed not only in Tucson but all around the country. Over ten-plus years their work has expanded to advocacy to make change in government and university policies, counseling for high-school students in how to identify and apply for scholarship opportunities, and training for educators and school counselors to encourage their support of undocumented students.

Some of that training for educators can involve the most basic of sensitivities. For example, Zobella told me that the state of Arizona recently began grading schools, in part, based on the percentage of senior students who have completed the FAFSA, the Federal application for student aid. As a result of that, some schools began to require all students to complete the FAFSA, going so far as to say that students couldn't cross the stage at graduation if they hadn't completed the application. But undocumented students are not eligible to complete the FAFSA, and many felt shamed by such a mandate. It is in those types of situations, and so many others, that involvement from Scholarships A-Z to create understanding and sensitivity can make all the difference.

And, each year, they have helped countless undocumented students who may not have otherwise had an opportunity for higher education. It is an impressive organization with an equally impressive list of success stories.

Those success stories include Dario.

But Dario doesn't carry with him any arrogance of success. He is soft-spoken and a bit unsure, knowing that the status and benefits he has now could disappear, including the opportunity to complete his graduate studies.

"People talk about the migrant crisis, and they think all migrants are in detention centers or wandering in the desert," Dario said. "We need to remind them of the migrants that are already here and need our support."

Dario is undocumented. Dario is a DACA recipient. And Dario is a human being with hopes and dreams, among many dreamers, just as my great grandparents were.

You may say I'm a dreamer, but I'm not the only one. I hope someday you'll join us, and the world will live as one.

Border Song:
The Things That
I Have Seen
(January 21, 2020)

*That did not prepare me
for the things that I have seen.*
- Richard Shindell

Over the four days that I had spent in Tucson, I had gained a great understanding of the journey that migrants make and the many dangers along the way and of the process for seeking asylum and the small chances of success for those seeking it. What I hadn't yet experienced is a sense of what happens when a migrant is apprehended or declares intention to seek asylum and is placed in detention.

Those are the deeply challenging things that I've seen today through two different experiences.

I am going to change all the names in sharing the first experience, as I'm not sure it's appropriate to share the details of someone's story and asylum case. As you'll see in the second case, I'm going to do just the opposite.

I thought it was important to be able to visit a migrant detention facility during this trip. I am grateful that I was connected to Jon, a retired attorney who gives of his time, along with four other attorneys and about fifty other volunteers, to provide legal representation to migrants in detention. Jon made arrangements for us to go today to the Eloy Detention Center, about an hour northwest of Tucson, to meet one of the people he is representing. He also brought along a student from California, Mark, who happened to be visiting him and would serve as our interpreter, as Mark speaks fluent Spanish.

On the way to Eloy, he told me the story of Maria. Maria is 29 and is from Cuba. Several years ago, she was approached by Cuban authorities insisting that she join the Community Party. She refused to do so, and soon found that she was fired from her job. She continued to receive pressure, including visits from the police chief. She was ordered to vote for Community Party members in elections and resisted. She and her boyfriend were both assaulted. She was pregnant at the time and lost her baby. She continued to be threatened and prevented from employment.

Last April, she decided that, for her safety, she needed to leave Cuba. Cubans are only legally allowed to leave Cuba to travel to two countries, Nicaragua or Venezuela, and they are required to purchase a roundtrip ticket when doing so. Maria bought a ticket to Nicaragua. From Nicaragua, she paid off border agents to get into Honduras. From Honduras, she paid authorities to get into Guatemala. From Guatemala, she did the same to get into Mexico. In Mexico, she hid out for several months before finally making the journey to the U.S., where she reached the Nogales border crossing in September and declared her intention to seek asylum. From there, she was sent to Eloy to be held in detention, and an asylum hearing was set for last week, on a weekday afternoon. The hearing started a little late. Maria has a complicated and detailed case, and it took Jon a couple hours to present it. By the time Jon finished, there were only 20 minutes left until the court closed. The attorney representing

U.S. Immigration said that 20 minutes wouldn't be enough time to present his case. And so the judge said the case needed to be continued, and there wasn't an opportunity to place it back on the calendar until April. Maria, Jon tells me, was, and understandably so, an absolute ball of tears.

Jon, Mark, and I went to visit Maria at Eloy this morning. First, to be clear, "detention center" is a euphemism for prison. Eloy is a prison with the barbed wire, the warden, the uniforms - anything you would expect to see in a prison. We were not allowed to take any cellphones or cameras inside.

We were given a private room with a table with a divider in the middle. Jon, Mark, and I sat on one side, and Maria sat on the other.

When Maria came into the room, she was smiling, clearly happy to see Jon. And, when Jon asked how she was doing, her tears started flowing. "I don't understand why this is happening to me when it isn't happening to anyone else. It isn't fair." Jon empathized and told her that, unfortunately, this isn't the first time he's seen a case have to be continued, and that he is going to reach out to the court every week to see if there is a cancellation where the date could be moved up. Jon praised her for her testimony, and they reviewed some details of the case to see if there was anything valuable that could be added when the case is continued.

Jon also asked her what her days were like. She answered that they are miserable, as she wakes up every morning and goes to bed every night in a cell. She has no freedom. And yet the chance of getting asylum is so much brighter than the prospect of having to return to Cuba, which for her would be a sentence to a life of violence and persecution.

While a small percentage of those seeking asylum receive it, in Maria's case Jon is fairly confident. Even though she came through Mexico, Maria is from Cuba, and Jon said that there is much greater sympathy towards those seeking asylum from Cuba because of the U.S. government's negative views of Cuba.

So in three months or perhaps less, we hope Maria will receive a positive decision on her asylum claim. But until then, she waits every day in Eloy, in prison.

After we drove back to Tucson from Eloy, I walked from Jon's office over to the Evo Deconcini Federal Courthouse, where it was suggested to me that I go to witness a program called Operation Streamline.

Started in Del Rio, Texas in late 2005 and expanded to Tucson in 2008, Operation Streamline is a federal government program of mass fast-track criminal prosecution of migrants. Every weekday, a large group of apprehended migrants are brought into the courtroom, and within approximately two hours, all are given the opportunity for plea agreements to be sentenced and deported.

I was told that everyday people go to the courtroom to bear witness to Operation Streamline. Today, I found myself the only one there witnessing. I was both sad and glad to be there.

The feeling in Operation Streamline was a bit surreal. As I was allowed to enter the courtroom, a group of approximately 40 migrants were being led in at the same time, all in shackles on their ankles and shackles on their wrists attached to shackles on their waists. All were wearing headphones in order to hear a translator, since none spoke English.

The majority of those on the docket for today have been charged with two crimes - a felony of illegal reentry by a previously removed alien and a misdemeanor of illegal entry. A small group at the beginning had only been given the misdemeanor charge.

After providing overall instructions to the group of 40, the judge called up eight people at a time. And for each of them there was a very simple exchange, six questions long.

1. *Do you understand the rights you are giving up and the charges being made against you?*
2. *Do you understand the consequences of pleading guilty and the terms of your written plea agreement?*
3. *Are you pleading guilty voluntarily?*
4. *Are you a citizen of the United States?*

5. *I understand that on January __, 2020 you entered the United States from Mexico at ______ and did not report for inspection at a U.S. port of entry, is that correct?*
6. *How do you plead to the charge of illegal entry?*

Each exchange took less than 60 seconds, with each defendant having an attorney standing behind them. How much each has had the opportunity to consult with their attorney and how much they actually understood about their charges and their rights I don't know, but I was skeptical.

And, by and large, everyone answered the questions in the way they were expected to - *Sí, Sí, Sí, No, Sí, Guilty.*

As a result of the plea agreement, the felony charge was dismissed and each received a sentence, with most being 30 days in detention followed by deportation, although the days in detention for some ranged up to 180 days, based on past history.

And, after the first group of 40 were finished, another group of roughly the same size was marched in. 75 plea agreements in roughly 70 minutes.

Each was quick and simple and cold, but for one.

One of the first defendants simply couldn't answer the "How do you plead?" question in an appropriate way, as he kept responding "yes." He clearly didn't understand. He was held aside until the end and then brought back up front to the judge to see if he understood the choice he was being given. It was a long conversation, probably 20 or more minutes, and there was clearly great confusion for the defendant. When the judge told him that if he pled guilty, he would be sentenced to 60 days in prison, he asked if that meant that he was free during the nights. When she responded that it meant both days and nights, he asked if that meant it was only 30 days. He asked questions about being able to use a phone to call his family and what the food would be like in prison.

And, at one point, despite his confusion, he said the most poignant statement of the afternoon. "You know, we're Mexicans. We don't come here to rob you. We just come here to find work to support our families."

Eventually, the judge felt confident enough that he understood that she allowed him to enter his guilty plea.

I felt the slightest bit comforted that she took the time to try to make sure he understood. But I left not knowing whether the other 74 understood any better.

What I experienced today on the second floor of the Evo Deconcini Federal Courthouse felt to me like assembly-line prosecution for expediency that didn't do justice to the defendants and didn't pay honor to our country. To pay the slightest bit of respect to those who were brought together into the courtroom today in shackles, many of whom, as it was said, simply "come here to find work to support (their) families," and were taken out today with guilty pleas, I list their names below.

I came to Tucson knowing there were difficult truths to be learned, but today I'm not sure I was fully prepared for the things that I have seen.

Operation Streamline - Tuscon (January 21, 2019):

Esthefania Rosas Gregorio
Cesar Antonio Bernal Ayala
Fabiola Sanchez Vazquez
Gabriel Montes-Hernandez
Jesus Miguel Rojas-Melchor
Antelmo Ezequiel Garcia-Zurita
Luis Cortes Morales
Selvin Francisco Fuentes Fuentes
Jose Vicente Reyes-Hernandez
Ranulfo Panzo-Ecahua
Hugo Cardenas-Padilla
Jeronimo Panzo-Calihua
Victor Alexis Ulloa-Reyes
Javier Adolfo Lopez-Sanchez
Leobardo Morga-Venegas
Kelvin Sanchez-Escobar
Fermin Gomez-Aguilar
José Jimenez-Solis
Samuel Chacon-Lachica
José Luis Flores-Padilla
Fredy Rojas-Paulino
Eberlin De La Cruz-Villa Lobos
Ildefonzon Garcia-Pablo
Eliazar Ovando-Estrada
Carlos Galarza-Hernandez
Marciano Ortega-Sebastian
Javier Ramirez-Rivera
Pedro Mendoza-Galeana
Jorge Enrique Bawman-Gonzalez
Salvador Collazo-Santiz

José Mata-Jimenez
Javier Rodriguez-Matias
Simon Ramirez-Gutierrez
Gustavo Guzman-Castro
Ricardo Bravo-Martin
Abel Esquivel-Martinez
Juan Pablo Martinez-Hernandez
Jesus Roberto Alvarado-Bernal
Silviano Ramirez-Martinez
Antonio Lopez-Bibiano
Pedro Martinez-Martinez
Avelina Perez-Hernandez
Roberto Culej-Vazquez
Juan Daniel Gervacio-Alanis
Gabriel Rojas-Olvera
Isaias Hernandez-Diaz
Mauricio Reyes-Lopez
Ismael Guerrero-Cantu
Jesus Santos-Santos
Isaias Cortez-Morales
Felipe Correa Sosa
Omar Fortis-Hernandez
Abraham Fortis-Ramirez
Abigail Velasquez-Dias
Elmer Jacobo Ramos-Estrada
Fidel Perez-Hernandez
Hector Manuel Zurdo-Salala
Luber Nehemias Mazariegos-Gonzalez
Valeriano Briseno-Sinforiano
Eduardo Sales-Simon
Ervin Velazquez-Lopez
Francisco Mansinas-Gonzalez
Andres Juan-Miguel
Osvaldo Tellez-Alvarez

Will Moises Rivera-Arrazola
Carlos Bello-Loyo
Jesus Manuel Juarez-Martinez
Andres Ambros-Temich
Marco Antonio Lopez-Sanchez
José Antonio Chigo-Ambros
Julio Velasquez-Roblero
Joaquin Santos-Oropeza
Primitivo Ramirez-Caballero
Jorge Hernandez-Mendoza

Border Song:
Smile, Though Your
Heart is Aching
(January 22, 2020)

Smile, though your heart is aching.
Smile, even though it's breaking.
Although a tear may be ever so near.
- Charles Chaplin/John Turner/Geoffrey
Parsons

Getting saltwater in your eyes can burn like hell. And crying salt-water tears can be both sad and soothing.

I had a bit of both this past week. Opening my eyes to horrible circumstances faced by migrants on both sides of the border has been incredibly painful, and I've cried real tears, on more than one occasion throughout the week, with yesterday's visits to Eloy Detention Center and Operation Streamline being the worst.

I wanted a reason to smile today; and I found it in a program called Iskashitaa.

Amazingly, while so many people in Tucson give so much of their hearts and of their time and energy to support migrants from Central America, Tucson also has arms long enough and a heart big enough to embrace refugees from around the world.

Iskashitaa Refugee Network is one of several wonderful organizations involved in that cause, and their central program is a simple one, described by their motto: "Harvesting Hope. Empowering Dreams."

Twice a week, volunteers work side-by-side with refugees from around the world to harvest fruits and vegetables from local neighborhood backyards and farms, with the food then being distributed to the refugees themselves to assure access to and availability of healthy food, and the remaining food distributed to food banks, shelters, and schools.

I was delighted that volunteering with Iskashitaa was the last stop on my visit to Tucson. I checked in with their director, Barbara, this afternoon. Barbara, who has a background in environmental science and spent time working with vulnerable populations in Africa, was particularly sensitive to the needs of refugees in her own community and started Iskashitaa nearly twenty year ago. In her first year of working with Somali Bantu youth, Barbara was taught the word *Iskashitaa*, which is the Somali and Maay Maay word for "working cooperatively together."

Barbara introduced me to Nolan, a young AmeriCorps volunteer assigned to Iskashitaa who would be my guide for the day.

Our fruit-picking team today included Jama, from Somalia, and Zeru, from Eritrea, with whom I worked side-by-side, even though we don't speak the same language. In fact, Barbara gave me a language cheat sheet they provide to volunteers which included simple words in Somali, Farsi, Arabic, Swahili, Kirundi, Karen, Spanish, Nepali, Tigrigna, French, Amharic, Mashi, and Kinyarwanda. While there are some South American refugees who participate in the program (from places such as Cuba, Colombia, and Venezuela), Barbara would welcome Central American asylum-seekers as well.

Our assignments today took us to three backyards, gracious Tucson neighbors with fruits they would never fully harvest on their own. We harvested oranges, tangelos, and lemons, and I found myself caught up in the fun and climbing trees in ways that defied my fear of heights (and probably a bit of my common sense). Over the course of three hours, our team, along with a second team (which included refugees from Syria and Sudan), harvested over a ton of fruit.

And, it's not just about the harvesting. Those who participate in the program learn English-speaking skills. They learn how to navigate their way around Tucson. And they receive all kinds of support from the organization, from donations of toiletries to guidance in navigating the social-service system and finding legal support for immigration issues.

Barbara has built of community of refugees and volunteers working side-by-side, for the happiness and benefit of all.

After a week of sadness, I was looking for smiles, and I found them on the faces of

Jama and Zeru and the others that I picked oranges, tangelos, and lemons with at Iskashitaa today.

And, while my heart is still aching, this afternoon I, too, could smile.

> *(And to my old friend, Iain Matthews, who I know reads this blog, yes it was your beautiful version of "Smile" that inspired the title of this entry.)*

Border Song: Flying Home
(January 23, 2020)

And I'll be flying home, straight into your arms.
And I'll be flying home. Carry me on. Carry me on.
And I'm flying home.
- Jason Robert Brown

I'm sitting in the Dallas Airport as I write this, on my way home from Tucson. It's been an exhausting and emotional week. I am physically and emotionally spent.

And, as annoying as air travel can be, I know my biggest worries are whether a flight might get delayed a few minutes or whether the person sitting next to me on the plane will hog a little bit too much of the armrest. But I also know I'm going to get home tonight; and when I get there, there will be warmth and food and water and safety and comfort.

On Tuesday night, I attended a weekly meeting of the Tucson Samaritans. One of the first orders of business was to give reports on the water runs that went out this week. It felt crazy that I had to give the report from last Friday morning's trip - my very first experience during my week in Tucson - but I was the only one on that trip who happened to be present at the meeting.

When it came time to give a report on a water run that had gone to Sasabe, it was reported that the group had encountered a migrant. Yes, those encounters do happen. The Tucson Samaritans group found themselves with a migrant who had walked across the border about a mile from Sasabe, where the border wall ends. A teenager from Guatemala, he was confused, hungry, and, most importantly, scared. A guest who was on that water run strongly urged that they should take the migrant into the Tucson Samaritans van, but veteran volunteers with the organization explained that they can't do that. The Samaritans have to walk a fine line between providing comfort and risking criminal prosecution themselves for aiding and abetting.

The young Guatemalan migrant said he simply wanted to go home. The volunteers wrapped him in a blanket and gave him some food…and they called Border Patrol, so that he could be taken into custody and sent back home to Guatemala, the place where he had clearly spent weeks running away from.

I am taking a lot home with me from my week in Tucson, and indeed the weight on my soul far outweighs the luggage I checked on the plane. The things that I have seen, the images in my mind, are just snapshots of a tragic story that happens each and every day. Maria stuck in Eloy Detention Center awaiting her delayed asylum hearing. The mother and daughter at Casa Alitas separated from the father, sent to detention in Mississippi, whom they may never see again. The 75 migrants in shackles and their assembly-line prosecution at Operation Streamline. Those hiding in the desert drinking the water that we left in hopes that they might not become another Prudencia Martin Gomez. Looking through the border wall to the spot where José Antonio Elena Rodriguez was killed by a Border Patrol agent with 16 shots in 34 seconds.

And I am flying home thinking about the concept of home and what it means to those wandering the desert. What is it that causes that young Guatemalan teenager to risk his life running from Guatemala, cross the U.S. border, and just wish to be back home again. What is home for Maria, who fled Cuba amid political persecution and now wakes up and falls asleep every night in a prison cell awaiting her asylum hearing. What is home for separated families who may never be reunited again.

I am deeply grateful to and inspired by so many people and so many organizations that I interacted with this week - including Tucson Samaritans, Humane Borders, Casa Alitas, the Jewish Federation of Southern Arizona and their Jewish Community Relations Council, Iskashitaa, the End Streamline Coalition, Scholarships A to Z, Good Shepherd United Church of Christ, Keep Tucson Together, the Tucson Jewish History Museum, and more.

They are doing amazing work on behalf of all of us who care…and they are fighting an uphill battle in so many ways.

I'm flying home in comfort and safety, and I'm wondering how I (and we) can make a difference, by opening the eyes of others and by supporting their efforts. And how our country, which I love and honor, can be

the warm and welcoming home for others
that it was for so many of our grandparents
and great-grandparents and that I still so
deeply wish it could be for all that see it as
a beacon of hope and safety and, well,
home.

The young Guatemalan migrant may be on
his way home today, scared and confused,
to a dangerous place that he was running
away from.

I'm simply flying home.

www.ingramcontent.com/pod-product-compliance
Lightning Source LLC
Chambersburg PA
CBHW031216160726
47992CB00006B/2767